GEMSTONE
BUYING GUIDE